Stuart is a barrister at 6 Pump Court an[illegible] as a 'leading junior' in Licensing by The Legal 500 for 201[illegible], 2016, 2017, 2018 and in Chambers and Partners for 2018. He is a member of the Institute of Licensing (IOL) and is holder of the Professional Licensing Practitioners Qualification (PLPQ).

Stuart is well known as a licensing specialist and has real depth and breadth of experience in all licensing matters. He often acts for the United Cabbies' Group and other taxi associations in respect of taxi and PHV licensing law and practice. He recently represented the UCG (On behalf of the United Taxi Action Group) led by Robert Griffiths Q.C. in a challenge to the decision by the Chief Magistrate in June 2018 to grant Uber a 15 month licence. He regularly acts for other trade associations, both hackney carriages and private hire vehicles, inside and outside of London.

He appears both at licensing sub-committee review hearings in a range of licensing cases, appeals to the magistrates' and crown courts and also at appeals and by way of case stated and in judicial review proceedings and is frequently asked to advise on all licensing matters, including local government licensing policy and relevant legislation. He represents companies, trade associations, individuals, local licensing authorities and other responsible authorities. He is a regular lecturer on all licensing matters.

Alongside his licensing practice, Stuart also specialises in connected regulatory law, such as food safety, health and safety, environmental, planning and administrative law, particularly in the field of local government.

A Practical Guide to Hackney Carriage Licensing in London

A Practical Guide to Hackney Carriage Licensing in London

Stuart Jessop
Bsc (Hons), Dip.Law
Barrister-at-law, 6 Pump Court, Temple, London

Law Brief Publishing

Published 2019 by Law Brief Publishing, an imprint of Law Brief Publishing Ltd
30 The Parks
Minehead
Somerset
TA24 8BT

www.lawbriefpublishing.com

Paperback: 978-1-912687-07-7

For Mother,

who always believed there was a book in me

PREFACE

The London Taxi, or black cab, as it is often referred to, is one of the capital's prominent icons. It is relied on by passengers, both visitors and those native to the city, as a safe and reliable means of transport. Drivers are rightly viewed as having undergone a rigorous examination of their geographical knowledge of London and both the vehicles and drivers are understood to be comprehensively regulated and perceived as providing a high standard private transportation system. Unlike private hire vehicles, hackney carriages can ply for hire, by being hailed in the street and taking a fare without a prior booking.

Many London taxi drivers have felt under unfair pressure from internet or app-based private hire operators who, it is claimed, effectively ply for hire through their apps when they are not licensed to do so. Such a claim is obviously disputed but it has created a tension in the field which cannot simply be ignored. Indeed, it has featured in more than one case in recent years.

However, this book focuses solely on the London hackney carriage and so some of these cases are not relevant to this book. The aim of the book is to provide a practical guide to the licensing of hackney carriages and their drivers in London. It will be useful for the licensed taxi trade and those that represent them as well as to those that regulate and enforce the laws and rules that govern licensed taxis.

I am grateful, to Stephen Hockman Q.C, and Robert Griffiths Q.C for their assistance in various taxi cases over the last few years and to Darren Rogers, Director at Chiltern Law for his loyal support and help with this book.

The law, as I understand it, is believed to be correct as of the 1st June 2019.

Stuart Jessop
June 2019

CONTENTS

CHAPTER ONE
HACKNEY CARRIAGE LICENSING IN LONDON: AN INTRODUCTION

Hackney Carriages are the oldest form of hire vehicle in England and Wales with documented reports of a hackney carriage as early as 1621 in London. In fact hackney carriage is still the official name used to describe taxis. It has often been said that the law on taxi licensing is complex and dis-jointed. One reason for this is that Hackney carriages, vehicles you can hail or pick up from a rank in the street, are regulated according to different legislative regimes to Private Hire Vehicles (PHVs), namely vehicles you have to pre-book and which are often called mini-cabs. Another reason for this complexity is that the legal regime differs according to whether the vehicle operates from within London or outside London.

It is for these reasons that this book concentrates on hackney carriage licensing within London. The law concerning hackney carriages in London is also complex and is found in several different pieces of legislation spanning over 150 years.

It is common for people to use the term "taxi" to refer to any type of vehicle licensed for the purpose of taking passengers from one place to another. However, in England and Wales the law divides such vehicles and therefore their drivers into to two categories: Hackney Carriages and Private Hire. A hackney carriage is also referred to as a licensed taxi, taxi, cab or London cab.

The key features of a hackney carriage are; it can carry passengers for hire and reward; it can be hailed; it can stand on a rank awaiting a passenger; or it can be pre-booked. The vehicle itself must be licensed as must the driver. Perhaps the most defining aspect of a hackney carriage is that it can ply for hire, something which a private hire vehicle cannot do.

Indeed the exclusive right to ply for hire is a feature which is highly cherished by those who hold a hackney carriage vehicle licence and driver's licence and has been the source of many recent disputes between the London hackney carriage trade and Uber London Limited, a private hire vehicle operator. Such is the importance of this right to ply for hire that this book dedicates a chapter solely to the topic.

In respect of reform, at the time of writing, the Government had recently given its response to the Ministerial Working Part referred to as the Task and Finish Group on Taxi and Private Hire Vehicle Licensing (TFG). The Government's response was summarised in the following terms:

> *"Above all other considerations the TFG put the passenger at the heart of its thinking; we welcome and share this view. Government will take action where needed to ensure a safe and well-functioning sector which meets the needs and expectations of its passengers.*
>
> *The Government accepts the three key measures recommended to achieve a safe service for passengers:*
>
> - *National Minimum Standards*

- *National Enforcement Powers; and*
- *A national Licensing Database."*

However, with so much else occupying the focus of the Government, not least the United Kingdom's expected but as yet unfulfilled departure from the European Union, it remains to be seen if or when such measures will be addressed.

This book deals with hackney carriage vehicle licences separately from driver's licences, each having their own chapter setting out the relevant provisions including the power to grant, refuse, suspend and revoke such licences. As has been said, there is a separate chapter on plying for hire. The book then summarises the various criminal offences that exist in relation to both the vehicles and the drivers and finally considers decision making in respect of licensing of hackney carriages generally and appeals against such decisions.

The relevant statutes and statutory instruments are too numerous and voluminous to set out in full in a practical brief guide to the subject but in order to assist those unfamiliar with the topic the relevant legislation is set out below:

Statutes

- Public Health Act 1975, s 76
- Rehabilitation of offenders Act 1974
- Criminal Justice and Public Order Act 1994, s 167

- Equality Act 2010, ss 160-173, and s 149
- Policing and Crime Act 2017, s 177
- Crime and Disorder Act 1998, s17
- London Hackney Carriage Act 1831
- London Hackney carriages Act 1843
- London Hackney Carriages Act 1850
- London Hackney Carriages Act 1853
- Metropolitan Public Carriage Act 1869
- London Cab Act 1896
- London Cab and Stage Carriage Act 1907
- London Cab Act 1968
- Transport Act 1985, s17, s 10-13 and Sch 7, para 1
- Greater London Authority Act 1999
- Transport for London Act 2008

Statutory Instruments

- London Cab Order 1934
- Regulations for Enforcing Order at Cab Standings in the Metropolitan Police District
- London Cab Order 1972, SI 1972/1047
- Local services (operation by taxis) (London) Regulations 1986, SI 1986/5066
- London Taxi (Licensing Appeals) Regulations 1986, SI 1986/1188
- Licensed Taxis (Hiring at Separate Fares) (London) Order 1986, SI 1986/1387
- London Taxis Sharing Scheme Order 1987, SI 1987/1553
- London Cab Order 1934 (modification) order 2000, SI 2000/1666

In respect of decision making by TFL, the regulator for hackney carriages in London, the reader is also advised to consult TFL's website for its various policies and the Regulator's Code.

CHAPTER TWO
HACKNEY CARRIAGE VEHICLE LICENCES

The legislation relevant to Hackney Carriages in Greater London, for example the London Cab Act 1896, London Cab and Stage Carriage Act 1907 and London Cab Order 1934, refers to "hackney carriages", "cab" and "London Cab" but all use the definition of a hackney carriage found within the Metropolitan Public carriage Act 1869 at section 4 (MPCA 1969).

> *'"Hackney carriage" shall mean any carriage for the conveyance of passengers which plies for hire within the limits of this Act, and is neither a stage carriage nor a tramcar.'*

Requirements for Licensing the Vehicle

Hackney carriage licensing in London requires a two-staged assessment where both the vehicle and the proprietor of the vehicle have to meet certain requirements.

Licences are granted by Transport for London (TFL) and the management of licencing is carried out by the London Taxi and Private Hire Directorate (LTPH).

Section 6 of the Metropolitan Public Carriage Act (MPCA) 1869 makes provision for the granting of Hackney carriage licences:

> *S6 Grant of Hackney carriage licences*

(1) Transport for London shall have the function of licensing to ply for hire within the limits of this Act Hackney carriages, to be distinguished in such a manner as may be prescribed.

(2) A licence under this section may –

(a) Be granted on such conditions,

(b) Be in such form,

(c) be subject to revocation or suspension in such event and

(d) Generally be dealt with in such a manner,

As may be prescribed.

Section 4 defines that "Prescribed" shall mean by London Cab Order and that "London Cab Order" shall mean an order by Transport for London.

The grant of a HCL is further subject to the provisions contained in Section 6. Section 6(4) states that "a licence under this section shall, if not revoked or suspended, be in force for one year.

The London Cab Order 1934/1346 deals with the criteria for applications for Hackney carriage vehicle licences. Applications must be made to TFL/LTPH on a prescribed form. The form is signed by the applicant and in the case of a limited company or partnership by the senior partner or secretary, manager or authorised officer of the company. The order uses the term "cab" to mean Hackney carriage.

By virtue of Article 6 of the London Cab Order 1934, applicants must be over 21 years of age and comply with other criteria set out in Articles 7 and 8 of the London Cab Order 1934 as amended by the London Cab Order 2007. TFL/LTPH have a discretion to refuse the application and these circumstances are set out in Articles 7 and 8 and are set out as follows:

GROUNDS FOR REFUSAL OF CAB LICENCES

7. Transport for London shall grant a cab licence if it is satisfied that:-

(a) The applicant is a fit and proper person to hold a cab licence;

(b) The vehicle in respect of which the application is made conforms to the conditions of fitness from time to time laid down by Transport for London; and

(c) The requirements of paragraph 8 of this order as to liability to third parties are met.

CAB-OWNER'S LIABILITY TO THIRD PARTIES

8.-(1) The liability to third parties to which this paragraph relates is any liability (other than a contractual liability) incurred by the owner or driver of a cab, as a consequence of the user of the cab, in respect of

(a) the death of or bodily injury to any person, other than a person employed by the owner of the cab whose death or injury arises out of and in the course of his employment, and

(b) damage to animals or to property not belonging to the cab owner or cab-driver nor held in trust by him nor

under his charge or control nor being conveyed in the cab, and not being damage to any bridge, weighbridge, viaduct, or road, or any property thereunder.

(2) *Subject as hereinafter provided there shall be in force in relation to every cab a policy of insurance issued by an insurer approved by the Commissioner of Police which insures the owner of the cab and any other person who drives the cab with his permission in respect of any liability to third parties to which this paragraph relates : provided that*

(a) a policy of insurance or a security complying with Part II of the Road Traffic Act, 1930, as amended by any subsequent Act, shall be a sufficient fulfilment of the requirements of this paragraph in respect of so much of the liability as it covers, and

(b) any other liability to which this paragraph relates shall not be required to be covered for an amount in excess of £10,000 (or, in the case of a horse cab, £1,000) in respect of any claim or series of claims arising out of any one accident or occurrence.

(3) *The Commissioner of Police may, in any case where he is satisfied that the financial position of the owner of a cab is such as to enable him and the cab-driver to meet without insurance any liability to third parties to which this paragraph relates, or any part of that liability, direct that the requirements of this paragraph (not being requirements of Part II of the Road Traffic Act, 1930, as amended by any subsequent Act) either shall not apply in relation to that cab or shall apply with such modifications as he may direct, and*

in any such case those requirements shall either have no effect or have effect as so modified, as the case may be.

(4) *If the owner of any cab in respect of which a cab licence is in force fails to fulfil the requirements of this paragraph as to liability to third parties, he shall be guilty of a breach of this Order : provided that the cab-owner shall not be guilty of a breach of this Order by reason only of failure to fulfil the requirements of this paragraph during any period during which the cab is withdrawn from hire.*

If satisfied that no ground of refusal applies, and providing that the vehicle complies with the requirements as to its conditions of fitness for use and that there is appropriate insurance, the authority must issue a licence, Articles 8 and 9 LCO 1934.

The LCO 1934 as amended by the LCO 2007, articles 2,3, provide that:

"Transport for London shall grant a cab licence if it is satisfied that the applicant is a fit and proper person to hold a cab licence; the vehicle in respect of which the application is made conforms to the conditions of fitness from time to time laid down by Transport for London; and the requirements of paragraph 8 of this Order as to liability to third parties are met".

If TFL/LTPH approve the application this must be recorded on the application form and the form returned to the applicant. If it is refused, the refusal must be recorded on the form and the applicant notified.

The Presentation of Motor Cabs for licensing

> *The applicant for licence for a motor cab shall present the vehicle for inspection and testing by Transport for London within such a period and at such a place Transport for London may by notice require.*

Affixing of Plates

On granting a cab licence Transport for London shall cause to be affixed to the cab

(a) The plates and notices described in Schedule B to this Order (LCO 1934) in the positions required by that Schedule; and

(b) Such notices or marks as Transport for London may from time to time direct.

The said plates shall remain the property of Transport for London.

Once the application is approved it is then for the applicant to present the vehicle at a passing station nominated by TFL/LTPH. The applicant must produce for inspection, the approved application form, current vehicle excise licence and certificate of motor insurance and any other evidence, if required, of compliance with the requirements of Article 8 of the London Cab Order 1934. The public carriage examiner then decides whether the vehicle conforms to the conditions of fitness and is fit for public use and must issue a certificate as specified in Schedule A of the London Cab Order 1934. The plates and notices described in Schedule B of the order must then be affixed to the cab as set out in the schedule.

The certificate is then submitted together with the approved application form to TFL/LTPH who will then grant a cab licence for that cab. However, if further matters justifying refusal have arisen or become apparent since the approval of the application the regulator has a further opportunity to refuse the application at this stage.

If the public carriage examiner is not satisfied that the vehicle conforms to the conditions of fitness, or that it is fit for public use, he must refuse to issue a certificate and report the fact to TFL/LTPH, who must then refuse to grant a cab licence. However, it is possible for the vehicle to be re0examined and then the licence granted if it so conforms.

The licence is granted subject to compliance with the Metropolitan Public Carriage Act 1869, the London Cab and Stage Carriage Act 1907, the London Cab Order 1934 and all Acts relating to Metropolitan hackney carriages that pre-date MPCA 1869. Article 14 of the London Cab Order 1934 therefore applies:

> *FORM OF CAB LICENCE AND CONDITIONS TO BE COMPLIED WITH*
>
> *14. Every cab licence shall be in the form contained in Schedule C to this Order, and shall be in force for a period of one year unless sooner revoked or suspended, and shall be granted subject to the provisions specified therein and subject also to the following conditions :-*
>
> > *(a) The licensee shall produce the licence for examination at his principal place of business when required so to do by any police constable or Public Carriage Examiner, or by any person duly authorised in that behalf by Transport for*

London, and shall also, if so required, produce in like manner such evidence as Transport for London may require that the owner of the cab fulfils the requirements of paragraph 8 of this Order as to liability to third parties.

(b) The licensee, if he changes his address during the currency of the licence, shall notify such change to Transport for London within seven days from the date of such change and shall at the same time send or deliver the licence to the office of Transport for London, who shall endorse upon the licence the licensee's new address and return the licence to him forthwith.

(c) The licensee, if during the currency of the licence he changes the place at which the cab is ordinarily kept, shall notify such change to Transport for London within seven days from the date of such change.

(d) The licensee shall not deface the licence by erasure or otherwise.

(e) The licensee shall not employ or permit any person to act as driver of the cab when it is hired or plying for hire except a person who is licensed in pursuance of Section 8 of the Metropolitan Public Carriage Act, 1869, as amended by Section 39 of the Road Traffic Act, 1934, and of Part IV of this Order to drive cabs of the type to which the cab belongs.

(f) The licensee shall produce the licences of the persons employed or permitted by him to act as drivers of the cab for examination at his principal place of business when required so to do by any police constable or Public Carriage

Examiner, or by any person duly authorised in that behalf by Transport for London.

(g) The licensee shall at all reasonable times allow to any Public Carriage Examiner facilities for the inspection of the cab and the horses (if any) used to draw the cab, and their harness, and such facilities shall include free access to his premises, whether within or outside the metropolitan area.

(h) The licensee shall not remove or conceal any of the plates or notices affixed to the cab in pursuance of this Order, or cause or permit any person not authorised in that behalf by Transport for London to remove or conceal any such plate or notice., nor shall he alter or obliterate, or cause or permit any person not so authorised to alter or obliterate, any mark placed upon the cab in pursuance of this Order or by the authority of Transport for London.

(i) The licensee shall not knowingly permit the cab to be used for any illegal purpose.

(j) The licensee shall keep the cab and all its furniture and appointments in good order and repair.

(k) The licensee shall not cause or permit any person to appear or be carried on the cab by way of advertisement.

(l) The licensee shall not, otherwise than in accordance with the directions of Transport for London, cause or permit any object or any printed, written or other matter to appear to be displayed on the outside or inside of the cab by way of advertisement.

(m) The licensee, if during the currency of the licence he ceases to be the owner of the cab to which the licence relates, shall within 14 days of the change in ownership:-

(i) notify Transport for London and return the licence to Transport for London for cancellation, and before delivering the cab to its new owner shall remove and deliver up to Transport for London or a Public Carriage Examiner the plates affixed to the cab in pursuance of this Order; or

(ii) apply jointly with the new owner to Transport for London, in accordance with paragraph 14A, to have the licence transferred to the new owner.

(n) Throughout the currency of the licence two test certificates issued in accordance with section 45(2) (c) of the Road traffic Act 1988 ("MOT certificates") must be in force in relation to the vehicle as follows:

(i) The first MOT certificate must relate to an examination of the vehicle which took place not more than 14 days before the end of the day on which the vehicle was presented for licensing (the day of presentation being regarded as "Day 1" for those purposes); and

(ii) The second MOT certificate must relate to an examination of the vehicle which took place not more than 14 days before the end of the sixth month anniversary of the date of grant of the licence (the day of the sixth month anniversary being regarded as "Day 1" for the purposes of that requirement.

Transfer of Cab Licence

Paragraph 14A of the Order states that Transport for London shall transfer a licence from a previous vehicle owner upon an application being made in accordance with paragraph 14(m)(ii) if:

(a) The application is made in such form, and includes such declarations and information as Transport for London may require; and

(b) The new owner satisfies Transport for London that he is a fit and proper person to hold a cab licence.

Maximum number of people to be carried

A vehicle that can carry more than eight passengers will be classified as a public service vehicle under the Public Passenger Vehicles Act 1981, however by virtue of the Conditions of Fitness as currently specified, the maximum number that can be carried in a Hackney carriage in London is six.

Is a London hackney Carriage always a hackney carriage?

Outside of London, a hackney carriage is always a hackney carriage. However, there is no authority to the same effect in relation to hackney carriages inside London and the legislation involved outside London is different. TFL take the view that the vehicle is a hackney carriage only when it is working as such but some commentators have argued that the legislation suggests that at all times, whether working or not, a hackney carriage must be driven by a person who holds a hackney carriage driver's licence.

Limits

Unlike the situation in some districts outside London, there is no limit on the number of hackney carriages licences that will be granted within London.

Transfer

A cab licence can be transferred upon death of the licensee, to the deceased's personal representative or the proprietor's widow or child if over 21 and satisfy the conditions of fitness.

Fares

Transport for London and London Taxi and Private Hire can set fares for hackney carriages within London by virtue of section 1 of the London Cab and Stage Carriage Act 1907. The level of fare is set by London Cab Orders which are amended to reflect the current level of fares, see Articles 40 and 41 London Cab Order 1934. Fixed fares are allowed in accordance with Article 40A. Drivers must also accept payment by credit or debit card.

Taximeters

Every motor cab must be fitted with a taximeter approved by Transport for London, Article 35 of the London Cab Order 1934. Every taximeter shall be sealed and may be marked in a manner directed by Transport for London and no person shall place such a seal or mark on the taximeter unless he is authorised to do so by Transport for London. The meter must be set to the rates set out in article 40. This is different to the position outside of London, where the meter can be set to a lower rate, Liverpool City Council v Curzon Ltd (1983). However, in London it is nevertheless permissible for the driver to accept less than the metered fare or to stop the meter before the end of the journey. The fares set out in Article 40 of the London Cab Order 1934 represent the maximum fare that can be charged but discounts can be offered on those fares. Any driver who charged more than the fare shown on the meter would be liable to prosecution, section 10 Metropolitan Public Carriage Act 1869.

Article 36 of the London Cab Order 1934 creates an offence of removing or tampering with taximeters. No person shall, without the authority of Transport for London, remove or tamper with the taximeter fitted to a motor cab in respect of which a cab licence is in force, or the mechanism by which the taximeter is operated, or break, alter, deface, or otherwise tamper with any seal or mark placed on the taximeter by direction of Transport for London.

Article 37 creates an offence of plying for hire without taximeters or with taximeters not sealed. The offence is committed if the owner or driver of a motor cab causes or permits the cab to ply for hire without a taximeter, or with a taximeter that has not been sealed and marked in accordance with the directions of Transport for London, or, if the seal or mark is broken, altered, defaced or otherwise tampered with and if as soon as practicable and in any event within 24 hours, the cab is not brought or sent to the appointed passing station in order to place a new seal or mark on the taximeter.

Article 38 of the London Cab Order 1934 provides for the lighting of Taximeters and "Taxi" signs. Article 39 requires that the driver of a motor cab shall start the taximeter no sooner than when the cab is hired or at such later time as the driver thinks fit and that the driver shall stop the taximeter no later than when the hiring is terminated or at such earlier time as the driver thinks fit.

Article 42 of the London Cab Order 1934 allows for the carrying of luggage or packages without people at the discretion of the driver.

Equality Act and Accessibility

All hackney carriages licensed by TFL are 'designated taxis' under 167 of the Equality Act 2010 and all hackney carriage drivers must therefore provide mobility assistance to wheelchair bound passengers unless they have been granted an exemption certificate issued under section 166. Section 165 imposes duties on the driver of a designated taxi which has been hired by or for a disabled person who is in a wheelchair or by another person who wishes to be accompanied by a disabled person who is in a wheelchair. The general duties are: to carry the passenger while in the wheelchair; not to make any additional charge for doing so; if the passenger choses to sit in a passenger seat, to carry the wheelchair; to take such steps as are necessary to ensure that the passenger is carried in safety and reasonable comfort; to give the passenger such mobility assistance as is reasonably required.

Mobility assistance is assistance; to enable the passenger to get into or out of the vehicle; if the passenger wishes to remain in the wheelchair, to enable the passenger to get into and out of the vehicle while in the wheelchair; to load the passenger's luggage into or out of the vehicle; if the passenger does not wish to remain in the wheelchair, to load the wheelchair into or out of the vehicle.

Failure to provide mobility assistance or to carry the passenger or discharge any of the other duties in section 165(4) is a criminal offence, section 165(8). There is a defence, section 165(9)(b) if the driver can show that it would not have been possible for the wheelchair to be carried safely in the vehicle.

In *McNutt v Transport for London [2019] EWHC 365 (Admin)* a taxi driver who activated his taximeter prior to unlocking a wheelchair ramp to enable a disabled passenger to board the taxi had committed an offence under the Equality Act 2010, s165 (7). Switching on the taximeter amounted to making "an additional charge" because passengers were legally obliged to pay the amount shown on the meter, and he had sought to charge the disabled passenger for the time taken to board his taxi.

A licensing authority must issue a person with a certificate exempting the person from the duties imposed by section 165 if satisfied that it is appropriate to do so, on medical grounds, or on the ground that the person's physical condition makes it impossible or unreasonably difficult for the person to comply with those duties, section 166.

Section 168 of the Equality Act 2010 imposes duties on the driver of a taxi which has been hired by or for a disabled person who is accompanied by an assistance dog or by another person who wishes to be accompanied by a disabled person with an assistance dog. The driver must carry the disabled person's dog and allow it to remain with that person and must not make any additional charge for doing so. The driver commits an offence by failing to comply with this duty. However, a licensing authority must issue a person with a certificate exempting the person from the duties imposed by section 168 if satisfied that it is appropriate to do so on medical grounds, section 169 Equality Act 2010.

In deciding whether to issue an exemption certificate the authority must have regard, in particular, to the physical characteristics of the taxi which the person drives or those of any kind of taxi in relation to which the person requires the certificate, section 169(2) Equality Act 2010.

An exemption certificate is valid in respect of a specified taxi or a specified kind of taxi, for such a period as is specified in the certificate, section 169(3). The driver of a taxi is exempt from the duties imposed by section 168 if an exemption certificate issued to the driver is in force with respect to the taxi, and, the prescribed notice of the exemption is exhibited on the taxi in the prescribed manner.

Hackney Carriage Stands

Section 4 of the London Hackney Carriages Act 1850 allows TFL to make provision for; the creation and alteration of hackney carriage stands; to make regulations concerning the boundaries of stands and the number of carriages to be allowed at such standing; the times at and during which they may stand and ply for hire; and for enforcing order at such stands including removing any person unnecessarily loitering or remaining at or about such standing. Such regulations are made by orders which must be advertised in the London Gazette with a copy, signed by a person authorised by TFL, to be displayed to the public in the TFL offices and at each magistrates' court within inner London boroughs. Each copy is to be taken as a true copy of the original and received in evidence at these courts as if it were the original.

TFL may by London cab order, designate any standing or part of a standing for hackney carriages appointed under section 4 of the

London Hackney Carriages Act 1850 to be a rest-rank. This can be designated for all times or for such times of the day, days or periods as may be specified in the order, section 10 transport for London Act 2008.TFL may also prescribe the maximum length of time during which a hackney carriage may stand at a rest rank. Different maximum lengths of time may be prescribed for different rest ranks or for different times of the day, days or other periods. Such a rest rank shall have a sign displayed at the rank clearly indicting that the rank or relevant part of it is a rest rank.

The driver of a hackney carriage which is standing at a rest rank shall not be deemed to be plying for hire and, accordingly may not be compelled to drive his vehicle to any place by any person wishing to hire it. TFL can suspend the operation of a designation of a rest rank for such a period or periods as they see fit, if it appears to them to be desirable or expedient to do so.

Trishaws or Pedicabs

This particular subject area of taxi licensing is a good example of how the regulatory regime differs according to whether it applies to London or outside of London. Outside London the relevant legislation is found in the Town Police Clauses Act 1847 (TPCA 1847) whereas within London the relevant legislation is contained within section 4 of the Metropolitan Public Carriage Act 1869 (MPCA 1869). Section 4 of the MPCA 1869 defines a hackney carriage. It makes clear that a hackney carriage is neither a stage carriage nor a tram car. The TCPA 1847 does not define stage carriage and in R v Cambridge City Council, ex p Lane [1999] EHLR 156, CA the court held that outside London a trishaw is a hackney carriage. However, In Oddy v Bug Bugs Ltd, 12th November 2003, unreported), (Admin) it was held, according to the definition of hackney carriage and stage carriage in section 4 of the MPCA 1869, that in London, a trishaw was not a hackney carriage but was rather a stage carriage.

Suspension or Revocation of Licences

19.-(1) A cab licence shall be liable to revocation or suspension by [Transport for London} on any of the following grounds:

a) if the licence has been obtained by any misrepresentation, fraud or concealment of any material circumstance; or

(b) if {Transport for London], by reason of any new circumstance arising or coming to his knowledge after the grant of a licence, or by reason of the condition of the cab, is satisfied that a licence in respect of the cab in question could not in pursuance of this Order properly be granted to the licensee if he were an applicant for a new licence; or

(c) if the licensee fails to comply with any of the provisions or conditions subject to which the licence has been granted; or

(d) on any of the grounds on which a licence in respect of a hackney carriage might at the time of the commencement of the Metropolitan Public Carriage Act, 1869, have been revoked or suspended;

provided that in a case where more than one licence granted to the same licensee becomes liable to revocation or suspension under this paragraph, the Commissioner of Police, if he is of opinion that it would be contrary to the public interest to revoke or suspend all of those licences, may revoke or suspend only such one or more of them as he may think fit.

(2) In the event of the revocation or suspension of a cab licence, the licensee shall, within five days after a notice to that effect has been delivered to him personally or sent to him by registered post at the address mentioned in or last endorsed upon the licence, send or deliver the licence to the Public Carriage Examiner at the appointed passing station for cancellation or for retention during the time of suspension, as the case may be, and if so required in the notice shall bring or send the cab to which the licence relates to that passing station in order that the plates affixed to the cab in pursuance of this Order may be removed and delivered up to the Public Carriage Examiner; and if the licensee fails to fulfil the requirements of this sub-paragraph, he shall be guilty of a breach of this Order.

(3) On the removal of a suspension of a cab licence which has not expired by the effluxion of time the Public Carriage Examiner shall return the licence to the licensee and shall cause the plates, if removed, to be re-affixed to the cab.

CHAPTER THREE
PLYING FOR HIRE

The concept of plying for hire and a licensee's legal right to do so is perhaps the most significant difference between hackney carriages and private hire vehicles. Indeed it is arguably the main issue of contention that has occupied hackney drivers and private hire drivers both inside and outside of London for some considerable time and certainly, particularly in recent years with the operation of internet applications such as Uber. Hackney carriage drivers can ply for hire whereas private hire vehicle drivers cannot and therefore it is an exclusive right cherished and closely guarded by the former.

However, there is no definition of what is meant by lying for hire in the legislation, inside and outside London. Further, the courts have not defined it instead have focused on the particular facts of each case. There are, however, certain principles which guide courts in any particular case although the case law is not without its inconsistencies. As has been said before in earlier chapters the legislation governing licensing inside London is different to that pertaining to outside, however in respect of plying for hire the statutes are materially the same and the case law is applicable to both.

Legislation

Section 4 Metropolitan Public Carriage Act 1869, applicable to the situation inside London, defines a hackney carriage with reference to plying for hire:

> *"Hackney carriage" shall mean any carriage for the conveyance of passengers which plies for hire within the limits of this Act, and is neither a stage carriage nor a tramcar."*

Section 7 sets out the offence of unlawfully plying for hire in similar terms to section 45 of the Town Police Clauses Act 1847, which is the Act relevant to outside London:

> *"If any unlicensed hackney carriage plies for hire, the owner of such carriage shall be liable to a penalty not exceeding five pounds for every day during which such unlicensed carriage plies. And if any unlicensed hackney carriage is found on any stand within the limits of this Act, the owner of such carriage shall be liable to a penalty not exceeding five pounds for each time it is so found. The driver also shall in every such case be liable to a like penalty unless he proves that he was ignorant of the fact of the carriage being an unlicensed carriage.*
>
> *Any hackney carriage plying for hire, and any hackney carriage found on any stand without having such distinguishing mark, or being otherwise distinguished in such manner as may for the time being be prescribed shall be deemed to be an unlicensed carriage."*

Cases

There has been a series of cases since the enactment of the statutes which have addressed the issue whether vehicles which were not licensed hackney carriages were nonetheless plying for hire and therefore an offence was being committed. The cases concern plying for hire both inside and outside London.

Sales v Lake]1922] 1 KB 553 concerned a charabanc which had hackney carriage plates but was not licensed to ply for hire and which was used for excursions to Brighton. Tickets were sold and seats were booked by passengers. The charabanc then picked up those passengers in various public places. No-one who had not previously booked could obtain a seat. The Divisional Court upheld the decision of the magistrate acquitting the driver and company of unlawfully plying for hire. Lord Trevethin CJ at 557 said:

> *"In my judgment a carriage cannot accurately be said to ply for hire unless two conditions are satisfied. (1) There must be a soliciting or waiting to secure passengers by the driver or other person in control without any previous contract with them, and (2) the owner or person in control who is engaged in or authorizes the soliciting or waiting must be in possession of a carriage for which he is soliciting or waiting to obtain passengers."*

Avory J, referring to the judgment of Montague Smith J in the earlier case of Allen v Tunbridge (1871) L,R. 6 CP 481 said:

> *"As [the judge] said in [that] case 'plying for hire' is very different from a customer going to a job-master to hire a carriage, and I think [counsel] was right in his argument in that case when he said 'plying for hire' means soliciting custom without any previous contract."*

Cogley v Sherwood [1959} 2 QB 311 concerned appellants who conducted a business at London Airport for hiring out cars with chauffeurs which could be hired out on the spot or booked in advance. The appellants had desks at both the then terminals and the service was well-advertised throughout the airport. The desks were clearly visible to arriving passengers. The cars were parked on a standing on the roadway at each terminal. At the central terminal the public did not have access to the roadway. The cars had the appearance of being private cars with no indication they were for hire. The appellants were convicted by the magistrates of unlawfully plying for hire contrary to section 7 of the 1869 Act. That conviction was overturned by the Divisional Court.

Lord Parker CJ considered at 324 that: "today, as a matter of common sense, I do not think that anyone would say that vehicles belonging to the many car hire concerns are plying for hire in the ordinary sense of the word". Having reviewed earlier authorities, including Allen v Tunbridge, the Lord Chief Justice said at 325-6:

> *"In the ordinary way, therefore, I should, apart from authority, have felt that it was of the essence of plying for hire that the vehicle in question should be on view, that the owner or driver should expressly or impliedly invite the public to use it, and that the member of the public should be able to use that vehicle if he wanted to. Looked at in that way, it would matter not that the driver said: 'Before you hire my vehicle, you must take a ticket at the office,' aliter, if he said: 'You cannot have my vehicle but if you go to the office you will be able to get a vehicle, not necessarily mine.'"*

He then noted that some cases pointed in a different direction, but considered that it was unnecessary to go into them because, in all cases where it was held a carriage was plying for hire, it was in fact there and on view. He continued: "For myself I think that it is of the essence of plying for hire that the carriage should be exhibited". He considered that the cars were not exhibited in this sense. The only cars on view were at one terminal, "they did not appear to be for hire; they appeared to be ordinary private cars with private chauffeurs."

In his concurring judgment, Donovan J said at 329: "the term ['plying for hire'] does connote in my view some exhibition of the vehicle to potential hirers as a vehicle which may be hired."

Salmon J, also concurring, said at 331:

> *"But for authority, I should have thought that a vehicle plies for hire if the person in control of the vehicle exhibits the vehicle and makes a present open offer to the public, an offer which can be accepted, for example, by the member of the public stepping into the vehicle."*

He considered that it was quite wrong to conclude that a car-hire service which was the modern equivalent of the job-master in 1869 was plying for hire. He said at 331-2: "I do not feel compelled by any authority to find that a vehicle plies for hire unless it is exhibited".

In Rose v Weebeck Motors [1962] 1 WLR 1010, the defendant's unlicensed minicab, a distinctive red Renault Dauphine with the inscription "Welbeck Motors, Minicabs" on its sides and a telephone number and radio aerial on the roof, was parked in a stand in Walthamstow where buses turned round. When a bus wanted to turn around, the driver of the car pulled out of the stand and parked about ten yards away. A licensed taxi driver called the police. When the police arrived and told the driver he was not allowed to be there to ply for hire, he disagreed with them saying he had been there 50 minutes and his control had told him he was allowed to be there.

The magistrates found there was no case to answer in relation to an offence under section 7 of the 1869 Act. That decision was reversed by the Divisional Court and the case was remitted to the magistrates with a direction that they should continue hearing the case. Lord Parker CJ again gave thc lead judgment. He referred to and followed Cogley v Sherwood saying at 1014-5:

> *"Again, in Cogley's case this court held that it was essential before one could say that a vehicle was plying for hire, first, that it should be exhibited or be on view to the public, and secondly, that it should while on view expressly or impliedly solicit custom in the sense of inviting the public to use it. The fact that, if those conditions were proved, a ticket had to be obtained from an office or a booking made other than through the driver was immaterial. It is right to say that a further possible question, namely, what was to be the result if the obtaining of a ticket or a booking involved a vehicle other than that on view was left open. Reference, however, was made to Gilbert v. McKay [1944] 1 All ER 458 and in the argument to Foinett v. Clarke (1877) 41 JP 359 , which cases suggest that, at any rate in certain circumstances, that fact would not of itself prevent a finding that the vehicle in question was plying for hire.*
>
> *That the vehicle in the present case was on exhibition in the sense that it was on view to the public is undoubted. The real question, as it seems to me, is whether a prima facie case was made out that the vehicle in question was impliedly inviting the public to use it. Whether in any case such a prima facie case is made out must, of course, depend upon the exact circumstances, and I certainly do not intend anything I say in this judgment to apply to any facts other than those here. What are the facts here? One starts with the fact that this vehicle was of a distinctive appearance, regarding its colour, its inscriptions, its equipment*

in the form of radio communication, and its type. Secondly — and this is equally important — it was standing with the driver at the steering wheel for some fifty minutes in a public place on public view and at a place where buses turned round: in other words, at a place where many members of the public would be getting off the buses and where many members of the public would forgather to board the buses. Moreover, when requested to leave, the driver drove away only to return immediately almost to the same place."

The Lord Chief Justice then dealt with the argument on behalf of the defendant that the car was merely advertising the owners:

"It is perfectly true, of course, that the inscriptions were advertising the owners, Welbeck Motors, Ltd., and also saying, 'and if you ring up Welbeck 4440 you can have one of the vehicles that they hire known as a minicab.' In my judgment, however the inscriptions on and appearance of the vehicle coupled with the place where it was on view and its conduct during the relevant period were saying more than that. The vehicle was saying: 'Not only do I,' if I may personify the vehicle, 'recommend you to Welbeck Motors, Ltd., where you can hire a minicab, but further I am one of those minicabs and I am for hire.'"

It is unnecessary to refer to the more recent cases since they can all be analysed as examples of the application to the particular facts of the individual cases of the principle established by Cogley v. Sherwood and Rose v Wellbeck that to be plying for hire (a) the vehicle must be exhibited or on view and (b) while so exhibited it is expressly or by implication soliciting custom in the sense of inviting the public to use the vehicle without a prior contract.

In Newman v Vincent [1962] 1 WLR 1017 the court found that a minicab that had parked for 20 minutes before the driver was asked whether it was available for hire was plying for hire. Parker LCJ found that the fact that the minicab had a notice attached to the passenger-side sun visor was important in the court's decision as was the appearance and conduct of the minicab that it caused two people to approach it and ask the driver whether it was for hire.

In Vant v Cripps [1964] 62 L.G.R. 88, a car stationary and unattended outside the defendant's house where the car had a sign on its rear with the words "Barry's Taxis" and on the house a sign the word "Taxi" and a telephone number, was found to be plying for hire. This case should be contrasted with Sales v Lake above, where the court found that an essential principle of plying for hire was that the driver was present with the vehicle.

In Nottingham City Council v Woodings [1994] R.T.R 72 the High Court held that a private hire vehicle driver, when approached stated he was free to take passengers, was plying for hire at that point. Woodings was the driver of a mini cab licensed as a private hire vehicle but not as a hackney carriage. His car had a sign on its side saying "Fon-a-car". He had parked the car and, on returning to it, was approached and asked if he was free. He replied that he was and was asked the fare to a certain destination. The two passengers entered the car and disclosed that they were plain clothes police officers. Woodings was charged with plying for hire without a licence and was convicted. He appealed successfully to the Crown Court arguing that he had not been plying for hire, merely taking advantage of an opportunity when approached by the police officer. The High Court held, allowing the council's appeal, that if a car was exhibited as a taxi and the driver was sitting in it those were highly material considerations in determining whether the driver was "plying for hire". When Woodings parked his car in order to use the toilet, and when he was walking back to it he was not plying for hire but when he sat in the driver's seat and told prospective passengers that he was free to carry them he was plying for hire, given the appearance of the car and its location.

In Chorley Borough Council v Thomas [2001] EWHC (Admin) 570, a private hire vehicle was parked attended outside a pub. Someone had asked the driver whether he was free without having pre-booked and then entered the vehicle. The driver then asked where he was going and before setting off contacted the operator to book the journey. The High court found that this was a plying for hire.

0There are a number of cases where the issue of plying for hire was also considered and all appear to turn on their own facts although the principles set out in Sales v Lake and the cases mentioned above were followed; Milton Keynes Borough Council v Barry 3rd July 1984, unreported, DC; Ongar Borough Council v Baker [1989] COD 489; Dudley Metropolitan Borough Council v Arif [2011] EWHC (Admin); Gateshead Council v Henderson [2012] EWHC 807 (Admin).

A very recent case considered the issue of plying for hire in the context of an internet application, Reading Borough Council v Mudassar Ali [2019] EWHC 200 (Admin). The High Court held that a driver who could be booked via the Uber smartphone app was not unlawfully plying for hire under the TPCA 1847. This was so even though the app showed a map displaying icons of nearby vehicles. The vehicles were not exhibited for hire as described in Cogley v Sherwood as customers could not select specific drivers or vehicles. The app functioned like a minicab operator but replaced booking by telephone with booking by app.

Lord Justice Flaux giving judgment at paragraph 33-39 held;

> *"There was no unlawful plying for hire in this case for a number of reasons. First, the mere depiction of the respondent's vehicle on the Uber App, without either the vehicle or the driver being specifically identified or the customer using the App being able to select that vehicle, is insufficient to establish exhibition of the vehicle in the sense in which that phrase is used by Lord Parker CJ in formulating the two stage test for plying for hire in Cogley v Sherwood and Rose v Wellbeck. That requires not just exhibition of the vehicle but its exhibition expressly or implicitly soliciting custom, inviting members of the public to hire the vehicle."*

> *"....Second, it does not seem to me that the position is different because, as between Uber and the driver, the latter is a principal and Uber is an agent."*

> *"....Whatever the correct contractual analysis, in my judgment it has no impact on the question we have to decide. On any view, there is a pre-booking by the customer, which is recorded by Uber as PHV operator, before the specific vehicle which will perform the job is identified. This is all in accordance with the transaction being PHV business, not unlawful plying for hire. There was no soliciting by the respondent without some prior booking, as he only proceeded to the pick-up point after the customer had confirmed the booking and the respondent as driver had accepted the job. Whenever any contract was concluded, I have little doubt that this was not plying for hire, because on the facts found in this case, the customer could not use the*

respondent's car without making a prior booking through the App. As with the charabanc in Sales v Lake, the customer would make a booking to be picked up at a pre-arranged point. On the evidence in this case, all the Uber App did was to facilitate that booking.

This leads on to the third reason why this was not plying for hire, which is the character of the waiting. The respondent was waiting in his vehicle until a customer confirmed a booking on the Uber App and he accepted that booking. There was no question of his soliciting custom during the period of waiting. His vehicle did not advertise itself as available for hire nor did he do anything which would have suggested to the public that he was available for hire. Indeed, as the Chief Magistrate found, if a member of the public had approached the vehicle and sought a ride, the respondent would have refused to take such a passenger off the street without a prior booking through the Uber App.

The waiting here was of a completely different character to that in Rose v Wellbeck. Unlike in that case, the respondent was not waiting to solicit custom from passing members of the public, but he was waiting for a private hire booking via the Uber App. Putting the example given by Lord Parker CJ in Cogley v Sherwood of what would not be plying for hire into the context of the Uber App, if approached in the street, the respondent would have been saying: 'You cannot have my vehicle, but if you register for the Uber App and make a booking on it, you will be able to get a vehicle, not necessarily mine."

These cases seem to establish that the essence of plying for hire is that the vehicle in question is exhibited with an express or implied invitation to hire it. Further the character of the waiting appears important in assessing these two elements. This might include where the vehicle is waiting as well as the length of time it waits there. However, whether a vehicle is plying for hire will depend upon the facts of each case.

CHAPTER FOUR
HACKNEY CARRIAGE DRIVERS

The power to grant a licence

The relevant law with respect to the power to grant the hackney carriage driver's licence is contained within section 8 of the London Hackney Carriage Act 1843 (LHCA 1843) and section 8 of the Metropolitan Public Carriage Act 1869 (MPCA 1869).

Section 8 of the LHCA 1843 states:

> *"It shall be lawful for Transport for London to grant a licence to act as a driver of hackney carriages, ...to any person who shall produce a certificate as shall satisfy Transport for London of his good behaviour and fitness for such situation."*

Such a certificate is the DBS Enhanced Disclosure. Without this being produced, TFL is unable to grant the licence. Once requested TFL must issue an application form on which the applicant has to declare any convictions and agree to notify TFL of any future convictions. It is an offence for any person to make false representations or falsely answer any of the questions, Section 14 LHCA 1843.

An applicant is also required to demonstrate his right to remain and work in the United Kingdom, S8A LHCA 1843. TFL must have regard to guidance issued by the Home Office. Guidance was issued in 2016 entitled *"Guidance for Licensing Authorities to Prevent Illegal Working in the Taxi and Private Hire Sector in England and Wales"*.

TFL can charge a fee for both the application and grant of the licence, section 8(8) MPCA 1869.

Section 8(1) of the MPCA 1869 provides TFL with the function of licensing persons to be drivers of hackney carriages. Section 8(2) prevents the hackney carriage from plying for hire unless under the charge of a driver having a licence issued under the Act from TFL.

Section 8 (3) makes it an offence for any person driving a hackney carriage and also the owner of the hackney carriage (unless he proves that the driver acted without his privity or consent) where that hackney any hackney carriage plies for hire in contravention of the section.

Section 8(4) provides that TFL may send to The Metropolitan Police Commissioner and City of London Police Commissioner details of anyone applicant they are considering granting a licence to and request the Commissioner's observations which the Commissioner is bound to respond to.

Once the licence has been granted TFL must provide an abstract of laws in force relating to such a driver, the sanctions for non-compliance with the law and the driver's badge. The driver must then wear that badge at all times when he is working as a hackney carriage driver. And if he is ever required to attend before a court. It is an offence for a driver to fail to do either, section 17 LHCA 1843. It is also an offence to transfer or lend the licence to any other person or permit any other person to wear the badge, section 10 LHCA 1843.

Section 8(7) of the MPCA 1869 states that a licence shall be in force for three years unless it is revoked or suspended.

Grounds for Refusal

A cab-driver's licence shall not be granted to a person under the age of 21 years, and if granted shall be void, Article 24 London Cab Order SI 1934/1346.

TFL may, in its discretion, refuse to grant a cab-driver's licence in certain circumstances. Article 25 of the London Cab Order 1934/1346 provides those grounds:

> *(c) If the applicant fails to satisfy Transport for London that he is of good character and fit to act as a cab-driver,*
>
> *(d) If the applicant is disqualified by reason of the applicant's immigration status from driving a hackney carriage, or*
>
> *(e) If the applicant has within three years immediately preceding the date of his application held a cab-driver's licence and has, otherwise by reason of illness or other unavoidable cause, failed to act as a cab-driver during any considerable part of the period for which the licence was granted or, where he has within the said three years held more than one such licence, the period for which the last of such licences was granted.*

For the purposes of Article 25 (b) above, a person is disqualified by reason of his immigration status from driving a hackney carriage if the person is subject to immigration control and:

> *(a) The person has not been granted leave to enter or remain in the United Kingdom or,*
>
> *(b) The person's leave to enter or remain in the United kingdom –*

(i) Is invalid,

(ii) Has ceased to have effect (either by reason of curtailment, revocation, cancellation, passage of time or otherwise), or

(iii) Is subject to a condition preventing the person from driving a hackney carriage.

Convictions

It can be seen that by virtue of Article 24 the applicant must satisfy TFL that he is of good character. TFL set out on their website a statement in relation to its approach to convictions of hackney carriage drivers and applicant for such licences and stress that each application will be decided on its own merits.

All previous convictions, irrespective of age, sentence imposed or offence committed, remain live for an applicant for a hackney carriage driver's licence (except protected cautions and protected convictions) by virtue of the Rehabilitation of Offenders Act 1974 (Exceptions) Order 1975 SI 1975/1023. However, it is likely that TFL should only take into account convictions which are relevant to the application for a licence, see Adamson v Waveney District Council [1997] 2 All ER 898, a case dealing with licensing outside of London.

The case law on the effect of convictions on the grant or refusal of applications can be found in cases involving hackney carriage drivers in and outside London as well as Private Hire Vehicle Drivers inside and outside London as the legal tests are similar.

Neither the appeal court nor the licensing authority can seek to go behind a conviction. In Nottingham City Council v Farooq

(Mohammed) [1998] CLY 4865, The High Court held that Justices acting as a Civil Appeal Court are not entitled to review the merits of the respondent's convictions for theft and dishonesty.

However, although the court or licensing authority cannot go behind the conviction the circumstances of it must be considered and the fact that there is a conviction is not in itself a reason for refusing to renew or grant a licence, *Pinnington v Transport for London [2013] EWHC 3656 (Admin). The type of offence, the facts, any policy of the licensing authority on the effect of such convictions and well as other circumstances may all be relevant.*

In County of Hertfordshire District Council v Prosser [2008] LLR 274, QBD, the High Court held that the particular convictions in that case, contrary to the view taken by the lower court, were not minor, that all convictions were relevant and that no convictions were spent for taxi drivers.

Each case must be considered on its merits and the objective must be to protect public safety.

On TFL's website the following guidance is set out:

> *"If you have any of the following convictions, it's unlikely that your application will be successful. Before submitting an application, please consider:*
>
> - *Any conviction for a major violent offence (murder, manslaughter etc)*
> - *Whether you have more than one conviction of any type of violent offence in the last 10 years*

- *If you are still serving a custodial sentence, even if you have been released early on licence or the sentence was suspended*

- *If you have been convicted, cautioned or subjected to any other penalty for a serious sexual offence (rape, indecent assault, trafficking, possession of indecent images etc)*

- *Whether you have been convicted, cautioned or subjected to any other penalty for more than one sexual offence of any type, irrespective of age*

- *Whether you are listed on either the Children's or Adults' barred list*

- *If you have been convicted, cautioned or subjected to any other penalty for touting in the last 12 months or have more than one penalty for touting in the last five years*

Please be advised that this is not an exhaustive list, licensing decisions are made on a case by case basis."

Fit to act as a Cab Driver

The concept of being "fit to act as a cab driver" is similar to that of "fit and proper person" used in licensing outside London.

The concept of being fit to act or a fit and proper person has never been specifically defined. However, there are some basis requirements that appear obvious. The objective is to grant licences to those who are suitable for the role and to protect public safety whilst doing so. A licensed driver will hold the trust of passengers who at times may be vulnerable to those who might exploit that situation. For an effective private sector transport system to work there must be confidence in those who are licensed to operate that system. In addition to being safe, from the potential dangers of the road and from any other threat to safety, passengers must feel secure. Driver's behaviour should not cause any passenger to feel uncomfortable for example.

The following cases, although not dealing with hackney carriage drivers in London provide some indication as to the nature of the legal test involved. *In McCool v Rushcliffe Borough Council [1998] 3 All ER 889, at paragraph 891F* the court said:

> *"One must, as it seems to me, approach this case bearing in mind the objectives of this licensing regime which is plainly intended, among other things, to ensure so far as possible that those licensed to drive private hire vehicles are suitable persons to do so, namely that they are safe drivers with good driving records and adequate experience, sober, mentally and physically fit, honest, and not persons who would take advantage of their employment to abuse or assault passengers."*

In *Leeds City Council v Hussain [2002] EWHC 1145 (Admin),* at paragraph 25 the court observed:

> *"There is indeed no authority on this point, but as Lord Bingham explained in the passage in* McCool *that I have already quoted, the purpose of the power of suspension is to protect users of licensed vehicles and those who are driven by them and members of the public. Its purpose, therefore, is to prevent licences being given to or used by those who are not*

> *suitable people taking into account their driving record, their driving experience, their sobriety, mental and physical fitness, honesty, and that they are people who would not take advantage of their employment to abuse or assault passengers. In other words, the council, when considering whether to suspend a licence or revoke it, is focusing on the impact of the licence holder's vehicle and character on members of the public and in particular, but not exclusively, on the potential users of those vehicles."*

In *The Queen (on the application of Delta Merseyside Limited, Uber Britania Limited) v Knowsley Metropolitan Borough Council [2018] EWHC 757 (Admin),* at paragraphs 43 and 45 the court held:

> *"I accept that the phrase "fit and proper person" in this context refers to the personal characteristics and professional qualifications of the driver and not to his or her work preferences and visibility.*
>
> *In none of the cases cited to me involving licences issued to drivers of hackney carriages or PHVs, has a court ever held that issues not personal to the applicant, such as location, are relevant to determine fitness to hold a licence to drive any licensed PHV."*

It is clear that the test focuses on the personal characteristics and qualifications of the driver and the impact of this on the public and their safety. *An informal test is often applied in the spirit of such an approach, along the lines of:*

> *"Would you, as a person with the responsibility of deciding whether to grant this person a hackney carriage licence, allow*

your son, daughter, partner, mother or father or any other person you care for to get into a vehicle with this person alone?"

If there are concerns about answering this question in the affirmative then further consideration should be given as to whether the person is indeed "of good character and fit to act as a cab driver".

However, it must be remembered that the test is wider than a focus on public safety. It is about trust and confidence. A passenger may well be safe in the company of a particular driver but, because of inappropriate behaviour, or language for example, may not feel safe. It is submitted that the test is therefore wider than an actual threat to safety.

Other Requirements and Limitations

The applicant for a hackney carriage driver's licence in London will need to pass a very difficult examination in respect of the geography of London, commonly known as "The Knowledge". In additions, he will have to pass a TFL driving test and have a medical report completed.

An applicant may apply for either a "suburban licence" or an "all-London driver's licence". The former does not allow the driver to drive within the centre of London whereas the latter is not limited within the area of Greater London. TFL are also able to limit the type of cab that drivers can drive, for example, automatic transmission rather than manual.

Once granted TFL must issue a copy of the licence to the driver who must sign the licence and the copy. The licence is retained by the owner of the particular hackney carriage and the copy retains the copy. The driver must have the copy in his possession at all times that he is driving and when appearing in court, London Cab Order 1934. He must produce it for inspection on demand by any police constable or public carriage examiner or any officer of the court. The driver has to display a copy of his badge and the area he is permitted to drive the cab in together with other notices and marks that TFL may direct. The licensee must inform TFL of any change of address within 7 days by delivering the licence and the copy to TFL and must endorse the new address on the licence. Failure to do so is an offence, London Cab Order 1934, article 32.

A driver's licence is granted for a period of 3 years, unless revoked or suspended during that time.

Although the Working Time Regulations 1998 SI 1998/1833 apply to hackney carriage drivers it is only relevant to drivers who are employed and therefore unlikely to apply to most hackney carriage drivers, who are self-employed. Therefore there are no direct limitations as to how many hours self-employed drivers can work.

A hackney carriage driver whose hackney carriage is standing in any street or place and is plying for hire has a duty to take a fare, s35 LHCA 1831. The driver cannot refuse a fare up to 12 miles in distance (20 miles if commencing at Heathrow Airport) or for a journey not exceeding one hour, s7 LHCA 1853, London Cab Order 1934, London Cab Order 1972 and London Cab (No 2) Order 2001. There is no minimum distance below which a driver can refuse a fare.

A driver who refuses a hiring may be summoned by that person who has been refused for a failure to carry that person, s35 and s36 LHCA 1831. However, the driver will have a defence if he proves that the vehicle was already hired. Provided that the driver "in civil and explicit terms declare to any person desirous to hire such hackney carriage that it was actually hired", then no offence is committed, s36 LHCA 1831. Further, section 7 LHCA 1853 provides another defence if the driver has a "reasonable excuse". Refusal must not amount to unlawful discrimination under the Equality Act 2010 but it is submitted that it might be reasonable to refuse to take violent or aggressive persons or those who are drunk.

However, a cruising hackney carriage which is plying for hire does not have to stop and take a passenger who hails him in the street, *Hunt v Morgan [1948] 2 All ER 1065, QBD.*

Fares

TFL set fares through the London Cab Order 1934 using the provisions in section 1 of the London Cab and Stage Carriage Act 1907 (LCSCA). A journey beginning inside London but ending outside is subject to a metered fare unless an agreement is reached between the passenger and the driver before the journey starts or if the destination changes during the journey, or at any time. For journeys not exceeding 12 miles or 20 miles if beginning at Heathrow, the passenger cannot be charged more than the metered fare. For journeys within Greater London greater than this distance or for any length of journey ending outside Greater London, agreement can be reached between the driver and hirer to charge more than the metered fare, *LCSCA 1907; Goodman v Serle [1947] 2 ALL ER 318, QBD.*

All hackney carriages in London must have the meter set to the rate prescribed in article 40. A driver can though accept less than the metred fare or stop the meter before the end of the journey, the London Cab Order 1934.

If the passenger requests it the driver must provide a receipt, London Cab Order 1934, art 41. A motor cab can be hired to take packages or luggage without a passenger but the driver is not bound to accept such a hiring, London Cab Order 1934, art 42.The hackney. Section 10 LHCA 1853 requires the driver to carry a reasonable quantity of luggage for every person who hires a hackney carriage.

The driver can require a passenger to pay a deposit for waiting in order to guarantee that the hiring passenger will return but it is an offence if the driver then fails to wait and also if the driver does not account for the deposit in the final fare. The meter continues whilst waiting, section 47 LHCA 1831.

It is an offence for a person to refuse to pay a fare and the sum outstanding can be recovered from the magistrates' court, s41 LHCA 1831. Section 1 LCA 1896 makes it an offence for any person to commit any of the following:

(a) Hires a cab, knowing or having reason to believe that he cannot pay the lawful fare, or with intent to avoid payment of the lawful fare; or

(b) Fraudulently endeavours to avoid payment of a fare lawfully due from him; or

(c) Having failed or refused to pay a fare lawfully due from him, either refuses to give to the driver an address at which he can be found, or with intent to deceive, gives a false address.

Such an offence is punishable on summary convection to a fine or 14 days imprisonment.

Carriage of Persons and Luggage

The driver of a hackney carriage must carry any number of passengers up to and including the maximum as stated on the vehicle, *s9 LHCA 1853*. No person other than the driver shall be carried on any cab in excess of the number of persons which it is lice censed to carry. It calculating such a number, an infant in arms shall not count as a person and two children under the age of ten shall count as one person, *Article 33 of the London Cab Order 1934*.

No person other than the driver shall, without the authority of TFL, be carried on the driving box or platform of a motor cab. No luggage shall be carried on the roof of a motor cab unless the cab is fitted for that purpose and is licensed to carry luggage on the roof. The driver and the owner are potentially liable for any breach of these provisions, Article 33 London cab Order 1934.

Lost Property

Article 51 of the London Cab Order 1934 makes provision for "Property Accidently Left in Cabs".

> *(1) Any person who finds any property accidently left in a cab shall immediately hand the same to the cab-driver.*

> *(2) Immediately after the termination of every hiring of a cab, the cab-driver shall carefully search the cab, or, if careful search is then impracticable, shall look inside the cab, to*

ascertain whether any property has been accidently left therein, and if he does not search the cab at the termination of the hiring he shall do so as soon as practicable thereafter.

(3) Any cab-driver who finds any property left in the cab or to whom any such property is handed shall, within 24 hours, deposit such property at a police station in the metropolitan area, in the state in which it was found by, or handed to, him, and shall truly state the particulars of such finding: provided that if such property is sooner claimed by the owner thereof and satisfactory proof of ownership is given, it shall be restored to the owner forthwith instead of being deposited at a police station.

Suspension and Revocation

The power to revoke or suspend a cab driver's licence is contained in Article 30 of The London Cab Order 1934/1346:

(1) A cab-driver's licence shall be liable to revocation or suspension by Transport for London if it is satisfied, by reason of any circumstance arising or coming to its knowledge after the licence was granted, that the licensee is not a fit person to hold such a licence.

(2) A relevant circumstance for the purposes of sub-paragraph (1) includes, but is not limited to, whether the licensee has been convicted of an immigration offence or required to pay an immigration penalty unless:

(a) In a case where the driver has been convicted of an immigration offence, the conviction is a spent con-

viction within the meaning of the Rehabilitation of Offenders Act 1974, or

(b) In a case where the driver has been required to pay an immigration penalty –

(i) More than three years have elapsed since the date on which the penalty was imposed, and

(ii) The amount of the penalty has been paid in full.

Once the licensee has been notified of the revocation or suspension he must return the licence, copy and badge to TFL within 5 days, unless he has requested a re-consideration or appealed the decision under section 17 of the Transport Act 1985. Article 30(3) of the London Cab Order 1934 sets out the provision and Article 30(4) provides for the return of the licence, copy and badge:

(3) In the event of the revocation or suspension of a cab-driver's licence Transport for London shall cause notice thereof to be given to the licensee, and the licensee shall, within five days after such notice has been delivered to him personally or sent to him by registered post or by the recorded delivery service at the address mentioned in or last endorsed upon the licence, send or deliver the licence and his copy thereof and his badge to Transport for London for cancellation or for retention during the time of suspension, as the case may be, and if he fails so to do he shall be guilty of a breach of this order.

(4) On the removal of a suspension of a cab-driver's licence which has not expired by the effluxion of time Transport for London shall return the licence and the copy thereof and the badge to the licensee.

There would appear to be limits on when a licence can be suspended. In *R (on the application of Singh) v Cardiff City Council [2012] EWHC 1852 (Admin),* the court, dealing with hackney carriage driver's licences outside of London, held that a licensing authority was not entitled to suspend the licence on an interim basis before revoking it. Section 61 of the Local Government (Miscellaneous Provisions) Act 1976 provided for a power of final suspension as an alternative to a power of final revocation; there was no power of interim suspension.

Although the case was dealing with cases outside of London it may well apply to hackney carriage driver's licences inside London. Its effect is to prevent local authorities from suspending a driver's licence pending further investigation as an interim measure. Therefore any decision must be to either suspend or revoke the licence as a final decision.

In Reigate and Banstead Borough Council v Pawlowski [2017] EWHC 1764 (Admin) the court made observations on Singh and the power to suspend, affirming its correctness. At paragraphs 22-26 the court said:

> *"Singh established that it was unlawful for a local authority to use suspension as a holding operation pending further investigation. Accordingly, a local authority could not lawfully suspend by reason of a criminal charge on a "wait and see" basis. If it suspended the licence, it had to do so by way of a substantive decision on the fitness of the driver to hold the licence. Once it*

was seen that suspension was not a holding operation but a substantive decision, it became apparent that suspension would rarely be the appropriate course where a driver was charged with a matter for which, if convicted, he would be subject to revocation of his licence. If such a charge merited action, and if the action was not by way of an interim measure pending determination of the facts at criminal trial, revocation would generally be the appropriate course. To suspend a licence because an allegation was made and then revoke it because the allegation was proved was contrary to the decision in Singh. That was not to say that, once a decision had been taken to suspend upon notification of a charge, no subsequent decision to revoke could ever be taken. It was possible to envisage a case where facts thereafter emerging from the criminal trial put a different complexion on the matter. The initial suspension would not necessarily rule out a subsequent revocation in such circumstances, having regard in particular to the fact that the local authority's powers were conferred for purposes of public protection. Any decision to revoke would be subject to a statutory right of appeal. Further, if it should later transpire, for example by reason of acquittal at trial, that the former licence-holder was indeed a fit and proper person to hold a licence, provision could be made for expeditious re-licensing, Singh considered (paras 22-26)."

A court can also revoke or suspend the licence following a conviction for any offence. Section 25 of the LHCA 1843 provides:

"It shall be lawful for any justice of the peace before whom any driver…shall be convicted of any offence whether under this Act or any other Act, if such justice in his discretion shall think fit, to revoke the licence of such driver,….and also any other licence which he shall hold under the provisions of this Act, or to

> *suspend the same for such time as the justice shall think proper, and for that purpose to require the proprietor, driver,...in whose possession such licence and the badge thereunto belonging shall then be to deliver up the same; and every proprietor, driver... who, being so required, shall refuse or neglect to deliver up such licence and such badge, or either of them, shall forfeit, so often as he shall be required and refuse or neglect as foresaid, the sum of level 1 on the standard scale; and the justice shall forthwith send such licence and badge to Transport for London, who shall cancel such licence if it has been revoked by the justice, or, if it has been suspended, shall, at the end of the time for which it shall have been suspended, re-deliver such licence, with the badge, to the person to whom it was granted.*
>
> *A magistrates' court that makes an order revoking or suspending any licence under this section may, if the court thinks fit, suspend the effect of the order pending an appeal against the order."*

Although the court has power to suspend the effect of the order it makes pending an appeal, there is not right of appeal to the crown court so any appeal must be by way of case stated or judicial review.

CHAPTER FIVE
CRIMINAL OFFENCES

There are a number of possible criminal offences that can be committed by hackney carriage drivers or proprietors. However, a criminal conviction is not necessary before TFL can take action against a licensee. Obviously a relevant conviction may impact on any decision in relation to a licence including suspension or revocation. A summary of criminal offences is contained below.

London carriage Act 1831

Section 35 provides that hackney carriages standing in any street, unless actually hired, will be deemed as plying for hire. The driver of such a hackney carriage refusing to go with any person wanting to hire the hackney carriage shall be liable to a penalty.

Section 47 creates a power for drivers to ask for a deposit if asked to wait by a passenger but also a penalty for driver's refusing to wait or account for the deposit.

Section 50 provides for a penalty to be imposed on the driver or proprietor for permitting persons to ride in the hackney carriage without the express consent of the hirer.

Section 51 creates an offence for any driver or proprietor to wrongfully take away a fare from another proprietor or driver who is fairly entitled to such a fare.

Section 56 creates an offence for the proprietor or driver to misbehave by intoxication, wanton or furious driving or any other wilful misconduct, injure or endanger any person; use insulting or abusive language or other rude behaviour; or assault or obstruct any police officer.

London Hackney Carriages Act 1843

Section 10 creates an offence for persons acting as drivers without licences and badges and for proprietors who allow it to happen and the transfer of such a licence or badge to any other person.

Section 14 provides for penalties for persons making false representations when applying for licences.

Section 17 creates a requirement for all drivers to wear their badge during their employment as a driver and when required to attend before any justice of the peace. It also creates an offence for refusing to produce such a badge for inspection when required.

Section 18 requires licences to be delivered to TFL upon expiry and creates other offences in relation to the wearing of badges and powers for the seizure of badges. It is an offence to fail to return a licence which has expired together with the badge to TFL within 2 days, section 18 LHCA 1843. It is also an offence to use, wear, or detain any badge without a licence relating to the ticket or to wear a false or counterfeit badge. Failure to return a lost badge that has been subsequently found within 3 days is also an offence. It is also an offence to use or wear a badge when the writing is obliterated, defaced, or obscured, so that the same shall not be distinctly legible.

Section 19 creates an offence of wearing a badge that has been defaced or is not distinctly legible.

Section 21 concerns requirements for the proprietor to retain the licence of the driver he permits or employs to act as a driver.

Section 25 creates a power for a justice of the peace to revoke or suspend a driver's licence where a driver is convicted of any offence and an offence for the driver and proprietor to fail to deliver up such a licence and badge.

Section 27 prohibits a person from acting as a driver without the consent of the proprietor.

Section 28 creates an offence and penalty for guilty of driving dangerously or other wilful behaviour.

Section 33 creates three separate offence of plying for hire otherwise than at an appointed stand, causing an obstruction by loitering or other wilful behaviour or allowing a person other than the hirer to ride in the driving box with him.

The London Carriage Act 1853

Section 16 places restrictions on advertisements causing obstruction or annoyance.

Section 17 creates three separate offences. Under s17(10 a driver who demands or takes more than the proper fare commits an offence as does the driver who refuses to carry the number of passengers marked on the carriage or specified in the licence for such a carriage or refuses to carry a reasonable quantity of luggage. Under s17(2) an offence is committed by any driver who refuses to drive the carriage to any place within the limits of the Act, not exceeding 12 miles (the distance has been extended from 6) or who refuses to drive for any time not exceeding one hour if so required. Section 17(3) creates an offence of driving a hackney carriage which is unfit for public use.

Metropolitan Public Carriage Act 1869

Section 7 creates a penalty to the proprietor for using an unlicensed carriage and for the driver unless he proves that he was ignorant of the fact it was unlicensed.

Section 8 A (8) creates an offence of failing to return an expired licence or a licence where the holder has become disqualified to TFL within 7 days.

The London Cab Act 1896

Section 1 creates a variety of offences such as hiring a hackney carriage without the means to pay the fare; hiring intending to avoid paying a fare; avoiding the far and after failing to pay the fare, refusing to provide an address or providing a false address.

The London Cab Order 1934

Article 14 creates several offences n respect of the licence and conditions to be complied with in respect of the licence.

Article 15 creates an offence of obtaining a licence by false statements or by withholding information. If any person for the purpose of obtaining the grant of a cab licence to himself or to any other person knowingly makes any false statement or withholds any material information, he shall be guilty of a breach of this Order.

Article 16 creates an offence of plying for hire without plates, etc, or with plates, etc, defaced. Subsection (1) states:

> *(1) If the owner of a cab, or, where the owner is a firm or company, the person holding the licence in respect of the cab on its behalf, causes or permits the cab to ply for hire.*
>
> *(a) Without any of the plates or notices affixed thereto in pursuance of this Order, or with any such plate or notice so defaced that any figure thereon is illegible, or*
>
> *(b) Without any of the marks placed thereupon in pursuance of this Order or by the authority of Transport for London, or with any such mark so obliterated, or indistinct that any material particular thereon is illegible,*
>
> *he Shall be guilty of a breach of this Order.*

Article 18 creates an offence for any person having in their possession any altered or irregular or counterfeit cab licence, plate notice or mark without lawful authority.

Article 21 makes provision for cab licences to be surrendered on expiry and plates removed. The owner of a cab, or where the owner is a firm or company, the person holding the licence in respect of the cab on its behalf, shall, not later than three days after the expiration of the period for which the licence in respect of the cab was granted, deliver up the licence and the plates affixed to the cab in pursuance of this Order to Transport for London or a Public Carriage Examiner, and if he fails to do so he shall be guilty of a breach of this Order.

Article 22 states: "Where a cab licence is held by any person on behalf of a firm or company, both that person and the firm or company, as the case may be, shall be deemed to be the licensee in respect of that licence, and shall as such be liable for any breach of this Order or any failure to comply with any of the provisions or conditions subject to which the licence is granted.

Articles 27 to 29 contain various offences in relation to the driver's licence itself.

Article 31 provides for breaches of the terms and conditions of a Cab-driver's licence. If the holder of a cab-driver's licence: drives a cab of any type which by the terms of his licence he is not permitted to drive (not being a cab which is withdrawn from hire), or plies for hire with a cab or permits the cab to be hired in any part of the metropolitan area in which by a condition attached to his licence he is prohibited from plying for hire with a cab, he shall be guilty of a breach of this order.

Article 32 provides for an offence of failing to notify a change of address within 7 days and deliver or send his licence to TFL.

Article 33 prohibits persons being carried in any cab in excess of the number of persons it is licensed to carry and otherwise regulates the carriage of persons and luggage.

Article 36 concerns the removal of or tampering with taximeters which by virtue of article 35 must be fitted to the cab.

Article 37 creates an offence of plying for hire without a taximeter or with a taximeter that otherwise does not comply with the regulations.

Article 38 and 39 concern failures in respect of taximeters, in respect of their illumination, activation and termination at the end of hiring.

Article 51 deals with offences in respect of lost property and searching the can to check for lost property.

CHAPTER SIX
DECISION MAKING

TFL is responsible for hackney carriage and private hire licensing in London. It is a body corporate created by section 154 of the Greater London Authority Act 1999. It has a board, chaired by the Mayor of London. TFL derives its powers in respect of licensing of hackney carriages and private hire vehicles from the London Hackney Carriages Act (LHCA) 1843, 1850, 1853, the Metropolitan Public Carriage Act (MPCA), the London Cab and Stage Carriage Act 1907 (LCSCA), the London Cab Act 1968 (LCA), and the Private Hire Vehicles (London) Act 1998 (PHVA). The board can make regulations and is the decision-maker in respect of hackney carriages and private hire vehicles in London. TFL discharges its functions through London Taxi and Private Hire (LTPH) which was formerly known as the Public Carriage Office.

The grant, refusal, revocation or suspension or decision to take any action in respect of a hackney carriage licence is not a civil law or criminal law decision. It is an administrative function performed by an officer on behalf of TFL. Such decision used to be seen as quasi-judicial but the correct view is that they are administrative but any appeal in a court would be a judicial function, *R (on the application of Hope and Glory) v Westminster Magistrates' Court and Westminster City Council [2011] EWCA Civ 31.*

However, TFL must act fairly in making its decisions. One way that this fairness is achieved is by recognising that a person has a right to know the complaint or issue against him and the right to be heard in respect of it. This must be even more obvious when one is considering decisions to refuse a licence, revoke, suspend or to take other action against a licensee or prospective licensee. This will mean that the person concerned should be given the opportunity of making representations. There is no statutory right for an oral hearing and many issues will be dealt with by way of written notification of the matter under consideration with an opportunity for the person concerned to provide written representations. Any oral hearing would be at the discretion of any licensing authority and it is therefore master of its own procedure.

Of great importance to the decision-making process is that the person affected by any decision must know the allegation he faces, *R v Assistant Metropolitan Police Commissioner, ex parte Howell [1986] RTR 52, CA*. This must be particularly so where the decision goes to someone's livelihood, *R v Metropolitan Police Commissioner, ex parte Phillips (10 November 1987, unreported), QBD*.

However, this doesn't mean that he necessarily needs to know all the details or have such information in witness statement form. He is entitled to sufficient information or the substance of the complaint against him and answer it, *R v Assistant Metropolitan Police Commissioner, ex parte Davidson (2 December 1992, unreported), QBD*.

The complaint does not have to be proved to the criminal standard so that the fact that there might be an absence of any complaint which resulted in a caution or conviction doesn't matter necessarily.

The other important criteria of a fair decision is the rule against bias, including the rule that no person should be a judge in their own cause. TFL publishes a code of conduct on its website and says, "We will have in place arrangements and mechanisms to ensure that all codes of conduct continue to operate in practice, to ensure that Board members and employees are not influenced by prejudice, bias or conflicts of interest in dealing with stakeholders."

If as a result of an allegation of bias or predetermination there is an issue about the validity of a decision of a relevant authority and it is relevant whether the decision-maker had or appeared to have had a closed mind when making the decision, he is not to be taken to have had a closed mind just because of what he might have done before the decision was made, which directly or indirectly indicated what view the decision-maker would take.

The test for apparent bias is whether a fair-minded observer with knowledge of the circumstances, would conclude that there was a real possibility that the tribunal (or decision-maker as it relates to licencing) was biased, Porter v Magill [2002] 1 A.C. 357. In such cases an absence of knowledge of the circumstances alleged to constitute bias is an answer to the claim, by reason of the principle that nobody could fairly consider a decision-maker biased by reference to circumstances of which they were unaware.

The test for presumed actual bias arises where a decision-maker or their spouse or partner has a direct personal interest, which is more than De Minimis, in the outcome of the decision, Locabail (UK) Ltd. V Bayfield Properties Ltd [2000] QB 451 (CA).

TFL is entitled to set policies, although there is no statutory duty to do so, and once set they should have regard to those policies. Policy forms an important part of licensing decisions and should provide guidance and consistency although does not bind any authority. Each case must be decided on its merits and a policy must not preclude the decision-maker from fairly judging all the issues which are relevant to each individual case, *Stringer v Minister of Housing and Local Government [1970] 1 WLR 1281. Policies must not be applied blindly and routinely without the possibility of exception, R (on the application of Westminster City Council) v Middlesex Crown Court and Chorian plc and proud [2002] EWHC 1104 (Admin).*

In R (on the application of Singh) v Cardiff City Council [2012] EWHC 1852 (Admin) LLR 108, the court considered whether the application of a policy amounted to a fetter on the discretion of the local authority in dealing with hackney carriage and private hire drivers within a penalty points scheme aimed at disciplining drivers for various infringements. The scheme operated so that as soon as a predetermined level of points was reached the licence was automatically revoked. The court held the scheme to be unlawful because there had been no application of discretion to the decision and in particular there was no consideration of suspension rather than revocation.

There is some persuasive authority for contending that local authorities and TFL could adopt an absolute policy. This is where, in certain circumstances, the licence will not be granted, see David Nicholds, Michael Hancock, Christian Thorpe v Security Industry Authority v Secretary of State for the Home Department [2006] EWHC 1792 (Admin), although this case was dealing with an entirely different statutory regime where there was a statutory basis for the absolute rule.

TFL is perfectly entitled to amend its policies even if they make their subsequent decisions stricter.

TFL must also have regard to the Regulator's Code. The code places six duties upon regulators namely:

(1) Regulators should carry out their activities in a way that supports those they regulate to comply and grow;

(2) Regulators should provide simple and straightforward ways to engage with those they regulate and hear their views;

(3) Regulators should base their regulatory activities on risk;

(4) Regulators should share information about compliance and risk;

(5) Regulators should ensure clear information, guidance and advice is available to help those they regulate meet their responsibilities to comply;

(6) Regulators should ensure that their approach to their regulatory activities is transparent.

Hearings

Hearings will be before an officer rather than a committee which would likely be the case outside London. However, the exercise must be fair and that would include the allegations, any evidence as well as the rules and policies that apply in that particular case being brought to the attention of the person in question. There is no requirement that the hearing be in public. Neither the criminal or civil rules apply. It is important to remember that the decision is administrative and evidence does not have to be of the type adduced in courts.

Hearsay evidence is admissible where it can be fairly regarded as reliable. In McCool v Rushcliffe Borough Council [1998] 3 ALL

ER 889, QBD, in a case dealing with taxis outside London, Bingham LCJ said:

> *"It is common ground that in reaching their decision the justices were entitled to rely on hearsay evidence. That in my judgment is clear from section 51(1) (a) of the Act and also from Kavanagh v Chief Constable of Devon and Cornwall [1974] 2 ALL ER 697, CA, it is also in my judgment plain from the judgment of Pill J in Westminster City Council v Zestfair [1990] 88 LGR 288, DC. I conclude that, in reaching their respective decisions, the Borough Council and the justices were entitled to rely on evidential material which might reasonably and possibly influence the making of a responsible judgment in good faith on the question in issue. Some evidence such as gossip, speculation and unsubstantiated innuendo would rightly be disregarded. Other evidence, even if hearsay, might by its source, nature and inherent probability carry a greater degree of credibility. All would depend on the particular facts and circumstances."*

In *Leeds City Council v Hussain [2002] EWHC 1145 (Admin),* it was confirmed that hearsay evidence is admissible before the officer or committee as well as before the appeal court. The court also confirmed that the impact on a driver's livelihood of a suspension (or indeed a revocation) is not a relevant factor for the licensing authority to take into account. The court held:

> *"There is no authority on this point but as Lord Bingham explained in the passage in McCool that I have already quoted, the purpose of the power of suspension is to protect users of licensed vehicles and those who are driven by them and members of the public. Its purpose, therefore, is to prevent licences being given to or used by those who are not suitable*

people taking into account their driving record, their driving experience, their sobriety, mental and physical fitness, honesty, and that they are people who would not take advantage of their employment to abuse or assault passengers. In other words, the council, when considering whether to suspend a licence or revoke it, is focusing on the impact of the licence holder's vehicle and character on members of the public and in particular, but not exclusively, on the potential users of those vehicles. This does not require any consideration of the personal circumstances which are irrelevant, except perhaps in very rare cases to explain or excuse some conduct of the driver."

Therefore the focus is one of public safety and a driver's hardship in having his licence suspended or revoked is irrelevant to that issue unless it can be successfully argued, in the circumstances of any particular case, that the two issues are linked in some way. This was attempted unsuccessfully in *Cherwell DC v Anwar [2012] RTR 15.*

As with all licensing decisions as decisions of public bodies TFL must have regard to the public sector equality duty under section 149 of the Equality Act 2010 and section 17 of the Crime and Disorder Act 1998, and the Human Rights Act 1998 when carrying out its functions, implementing policy and making decisions.

Once the decision is made reasons should be given either at the time or more commonly in writing as soon as possible thereafter. Reasons are essential in all licensing cases and there needs to be sufficient detail to enable the potential appellant to know the basis upon which the decision was made and for the licensing authority to be able to defend its position if appropriate, *R (on the application of Hope and Glory Public House Ltd) v Westminster City*

Magistrates' Court [2011] EWCA Civ 31. However, the weight that any appeal court gives to reasons given by the authority or the lack of reasons is a matter for the court and it can come to its own view on the evidence.

Fees

TFL can and do charge fees for both hackney carriage vehicle licences and driver's licences. The power to demand a fee comes from the Metropolitan Public Carriage Act 1869. Sections 898) (10) and (11) provide the power in respect of driver's licences. The provisions are identical.

> *(5) A fee of such amount (if any) as Transport for London may determine shall be paid to Transport for London—*
>
> > *(a) by any applicant for a licence under this section, on making the application for the licence;*
> >
> > *(b) by any applicant for the taking or re-taking of any test or examination, or any part of a test or examination, with respect to any matter of fitness, on making the application for the taking or re-taking of the test examination or part, and*
> >
> > *(c) by any person granted a licence under this section, on the grant of the licence*
>
> *(6) In paragraph (b) of subsection (5) of this section "matter of fitness" means—*
>
> > *(a) any matter as respects which Transport for London must be satisfied before granting a licence under this section; or*

(b) any matter such that, if Transport for London is not satisfied with respect to the matter, they may refuse to grant a licence under this section.

(7) Different amounts may be determined under subsection (5) of this section for different purposes or different cases.

(8) Transport for London may remit or refund the whole or part of a fee under subsection (5) of this section.

CHAPTER SEVEN
APPEALS

Licensing decisions are susceptible both to judicial review and by way of statutory appeal. In the case of hackney carriages in London, for both vehicle and drivers' licences, that right of appeal against suspension or revocation lies to the magistrates' court under section 17 of the Transport Act 1985. Section 17 sets out the right of appeal as follows:

(1) In this section—

"licence" means a licence under section 6 of the Metropolitan Public Carriage Act 1869 (taxi licences) or under section 8 of that Act (taxi driver licences); and

"licensing authority" means the person empowered to grant a licence.

(2) Where the licensing authority has refused to grant, or has suspended or revoked, a licence the applicant for, or (as the case may be) holder of, the licence may, before the expiry of the [designated period] —

(a) require the authority to reconsider his decision; or

(b) appeal to [a magistrates'] court.

(3) Any call for a reconsideration under subsection (2) above must be made to the licensing authority in writing.

(4) On any reconsideration under this section the person calling for the decision to be reconsidered shall be entitled to be heard either in person or by his representative.

(5) If the person calling for a decision to be reconsidered under this section is dissatisfied with the decision of the licensing authority on reconsideration, he may, before the expiry of the [designated period] , appeal to [a magistrates'] court.

(6) On any appeal to it under this section, the court may make such order as it thinks fit; and any order which it makes shall be binding on the licensing authority.

(7) Where a person holds a licence which is in force when he applies for a new licence in substitution for it, the existing licence shall continue in force until the application for the new licence, or any appeal under this section in relation to that application, is disposed of, but without prejudice to the exercise in the meantime of any power of the licensing authority to revoke the existing licence.

(8) For the purposes of subsection (7) above, where the licensing authority refuses to grant the new licence the application shall not be treated as disposed of—

> *(a) where no call for a reconsideration of the authority's decision is made under subsection (2) above, until the expiry of the [designated period];*
>
> *(b) where such a reconsideration is called for, until the expiry of the [designated period] which begins by reference to the decision of the authority on reconsideration.*

(9) Where the licensing authority suspends or revokes a licence, or confirms a decision to do so, he may, if the holder of the licence so requests, direct that his decision shall not have effect until the expiry of the [designated period].

(10) In this section [...]["designated period" means such period as may be specified for the purpose by London cab order;] ["London cab order" means an order made by Transport for London]

(11) Any power to make a London cab order under this section includes power to vary or revoke a previous such order.

It can be seen that the applicant or the holder of the licence, as the case may be, may require the authority to reconsider the decision or appeal to the magistrates' court. Such an appeal has to be made within 28 days of the decision being communicated by a notice, Regulation 2 London Taxis (Licensing Appeals) Regulations 1986. If the person is dissatisfied with the decision on reconsideration he has 28 days from that reconsidered decision to appeal to the magistrates' court.

Neither the Civil Procedure Rules nor the Criminal Procedural Rules apply although the Magistrates' courts Rules 1981 do apply. Hearsay evidence is admissible as much as it is before the original decision maker. The party wishing to rely on the hearsay must give notice to the other parties and file with the court not less than 21 days before the date of the hearing, Magistrates' Courts (Hearsay Evidence in Civil Proceedings) Rules 19999.The hearing is heard de novo or afresh. The court must place itself in the position of the decision-maker whose decision it is determining.

The procedure to be followed by the court is contained in Rule 14 of the Magistrates' Courts Rules 1981. However, the order is sometimes, by agreement, altered so that the Respondent starts its case first. The burden lies on the Appellant to persuade the court that the authority should not have exercised its discretion in the way that it did, in other words that the decision is wrong. The court must make its decision on the full material before it and is entitled to consider material which has arisen since the decision. The test is whether taking all the relevant material into account, the decision is wrong. The court must consider the licensing authority's decision and not overturn it lightly, Stepney Borough Council v Joffe [1949] 1 KB 599, DC; Sagnata Investments Ltd v Norwich Corporation [1971] 2 QB 614, CA. The court must consider the licensing policy when making its decision. In R (on the application of Westminster City Council) v Middlesex Crown Court and Chorian plc and Proud 29th May 2002, unreported, Admin Court Mr Justice Scott Baker said:

> *"In my judgment it must accept the policy and apply it as if it was standing in the shoes of the council considering the application. Neither the Magistrates' Court nor the Crown Court is the right place to challenge the policy."*

The court can dismiss the appeal or uphold it as it has power to "make such an order as it thinks fit".

There is no further appeal from the magistrate's court. Any further challenge must be by way of case stated.

Costs

The court has a power to award costs, section 64 Magistrates' Courts Act 1980. The issue as to whether such costs will be granted in favour of a successful appellant in the magistrates' court was dealt with in Bradford Metropolitan Borough Council v Booth [2000] COD 338, QBD. The court gave its judgment at paragraphs 22-26:

> *"22. It seems to me that the justices in this case misdirected themselves, first, in relying on a principle that costs should follow the event, that misdirection being compounded by their view that the reference in section 64 to the order being just and reasonable applied to quantum only. On the other hand, in my judgment the submissions made by Mr Blair-Gould on behalf of the local authority go too far the other way since to give effect to the principle for which he contends would deprive the justices of any discretion to view the case in the round which is in my judgment what section 64 intends.*
>
> *23. I would accordingly hold that the proper approach to questions of this kind can for convenience be summarised is three propositions:*
>
> *24. 1. Section 64(1) confers a discretion upon a magistrates' court to make such order as to costs as it thinks just and reasonable. That provision applies both to the quantum of the costs (if any) to be paid, but also as to the party (if any) which should pay them.*
>
> *25. 2. What the court will think just and reasonable will depend on all the relevant facts and circumstances of the case before the court. The court may think it just and reasonable*

that costs should follow the event, but need not think so in all cases covered by the subsection.

26. 3. Where a complainant has successfully challenged before justices an administrative decision made by a police or regulatory authority acting honestly, reasonably, properly and on grounds that reasonably appeared to be sound, in exercise of its public duty, the court should consider, in addition to any other relevant fact or circumstances, both (i) the financial prejudice to the particular complainant in the particular circumstances if an order for costs is not made in his favour; and (ii) the need to encourage public authorities to make and stand by honest, reasonable and apparently sound administrative decisions made in the public interest without fear of exposure to undue financial prejudice if the decision is successfully challenged."

Despite this case there is no automatic bar to costs being awarded against licensing authorities where they have not acted honestly, reasonably and properly, Powell v City and County of Swansea (30th July 2003, unreported) Admin. The principles set out in Bradford were approved in R(on the application of Perinpanathan) v Westminster Magistrates' Court, dealing with cash forfeiture under the Proceeds of Crime Act 2002, where the court reviewed a number of cases and concluded:

"40 I derive the following propositions from the authorities to which I have referred:

(1) As a result of the decision of the Court of Appeal in Baxendale-Walker, the principle in the City of Bradford case is binding on this Court. Quite apart from authority, however, for the reasons given by Lord Bingham LCJ I would respectfully

endorse its application in licensing proceedings in the magistrates' court and the Crown Court.

(2) For the same reasons, the principle is applicable to disciplinary proceedings before tribunals at first instance brought by public authorities acting in the public interest: Baxendale-Walker.

(3) Whether the principle should be applied in other contexts will depend on the substantive legislative framework and the applicable procedural provisions.

(4) The principle does not apply in proceedings to which the CPR apply.

(5) Where the principle applies, and the party opposing the order sought by the public authority has been successful, in relation to costs the starting point and default position is that no order should be made.

(6) A successful private party to proceedings to which the principle applies may nonetheless be awarded all or part of his costs if the conduct of the public authority in question justifies it.

(7) Other facts relevant to the exercise of the discretion conferred by the applicable procedural rules may also justify an order for costs. It would not be sensible to try exhaustively to define such matters, and I do not propose to do so.

41 Lord Bingham LCJ stated that financial prejudice to the private party may justify an order for costs in his favour. I think it clear that the financial prejudice necessarily involved in litigation would not normally justify an order. If that were not so, an order would be made in every case in which the successful private party incurred legal costs. Lord Bingham LCJ had in mind a case in which the successful private party would suffer substantial hardship if no order for costs was made in his favour. I respectfully agree with what Toulson J (with whom Richards LJ agreed) said in R (Cambridge City Council) v Alex Nestling Ltd:

12. As to the financial loss suffered by the successful appellant, a successful appellant who has to bear his own costs will necessarily be out of pocket, and that is the reason in ordinary civil litigation for the principle that costs follow the event. But that principle does not apply in this type of case. When Lord Bingham referred to the need to consider the financial prejudice to a particular complainant in the particular circumstances, he was not in implying that an award for costs should routinely follow in favour of a successful appellant; quite to the contrary.

42 I would also comment that there may have been a tendency to focus more on Lord Bingham LCJ's answer to the straightforward issue defined in paragraph 1 of his judgment than to the more nuanced propositions set out under paragraph 23. Ultimately, the duty of the magistrates' court is to make such order as to costs as is just and reasonable, subject to the constraint imposed by section 64."

MORE BOOKS BY LAW BRIEF PUBLISHING

A selection of our other titles available now:-

'A Practical Guide to TOLATA Claims' by Greg Williams
'Planning Obligations Demystified: A Practical Guide to Planning Obligations and Section 106 Agreements' by Bob Mc Geady & Meyric Lewis
'A Practical Guide to Agricultural Law and Tenancies' by Christopher McNall
'A Practical Guide to Crofting Law' by Brian Inkster
'A Practical Guide to Spousal Maintenance' by Liz Cowell
'A Practical Guide to the Law of Domain Names and Cybersquatting' by Andrew Clemson
'A Practical Guide to the Law of Gender Pay Gap Reporting' by Harini Iyengar
'Ellis and Kevan on Credit Hire – 5th Edition' by Aidan Ellis & Tim Kevan
'Artificial Intelligence – The Practical Legal Issues' by John Buyers
'A Practical Guide to the Rights of Grandparents in Children Proceedings' by Stuart Barlow
'NHS Whistleblowing and the Law' by Joseph England
'Employment Law and the Gig Economy' by Nigel Mackay & Annie Powell
'A Practical Guide to the General Data Protection Regulation (GDPR)' by Keith Markham
'A Practical Guide to Noise Induced Hearing Loss (NIHL) Claims' by Andrew Mckie, Ian Skeate, Gareth McAloon
'An Introduction to Beauty Negligence Claims – A Practical Guide for the Personal Injury Practitioner' by Greg Almond
'Intercompany Agreements for Transfer Pricing Compliance' by Paul Sutton
'Zen and the Art of Mediation' by Martin Plowman
'A Practical Guide to the SRA Principles, Individual and Law Firm Codes of Conduct 2019 – What Every Law Firm Needs to Know' by Paul Bennett

‘A Practical Guide to Licensing Law for Commercial Property Lawyers’ by Niall McCann & Richard Williams
‘A Practical Guide to Adoption for Family Lawyers’ by Graham Pegg
‘Essential Motor Finance Law for the Busy Practitioner’ by Richard Humphreys
‘A Practical Guide to Industrial Disease Claims’ by Andrew Mckie & Ian Skeate
‘A Practical Guide to the Law of Armed Conflict’ by Jo Morris & Libby Anderson
‘A Practical Guide to Redundancy’ by Philip Hyland
‘A Practical Guide to Vicarious Liability’ by Mariel Irvine
‘A Practical Guide to Claims Arising from Delays in Diagnosing Cancer’ by Bella Webb
‘A Practical Guide to Applications for Landlord’s Consent and Variation of Leases’ by Mark Shelton
‘A Practical Guide to Relief from Sanctions Post-Mitchell and Denton’ by Peter Causton
‘Butler’s Equine Tax Planning: 2nd Edition’ by Julie Butler
‘A Practical Guide to Equity Release for Advisors’ by Paul Sams
‘A Practical Guide to Unlawful Eviction and Harassment’ by Stephanie Lovegrove
‘A Practical Guide to the Law Relating to Food’ by Ian Thomas
‘A Practical Guide to the Ending of Assured Shorthold Tenancies’ by Elizabeth Dwomoh
‘A Practical Guide to Financial Services Claims’ by Chris Hegarty
‘The Law of Houses in Multiple Occupation: A Practical Guide to HMO Proceedings’ by Julian Hunt
‘A Practical Guide to Unlawful Eviction and Harassment’ by Stephanie Lovegrove
‘A Practical Guide to Solicitor and Client Costs’ by Robin Dunne
‘A Practical Guide to Wrongful Conception, Wrongful Birth and Wrongful Life Claims’ by Rebecca Greenstreet
‘Occupiers, Highways and Defective Premises Claims: A Practical Guide Post-Jackson – 2nd Edition’ by Andrew Mckie
‘A Practical Guide to Financial Ombudsman Service Claims’ by Adam Temple & Robert Scrivenor

‘A Practical Guide to the Law of Enfranchisement and Lease Extension’ by Paul Sams
‘A Practical Guide to Marketing for Lawyers – 2nd Edition’ by Catherine Bailey & Jennet Ingram
'A Practical Guide to Advising Schools on Employment Law' by Jonathan Holden
'Certificates of Lawful Use and Development: A Guide to Making and Determining Applications' by Bob Mc Geady & Meyric Lewis
'A Practical Guide to the Law of Dilapidations' by Mark Shelton
‘A Practical Guide to the 2018 Jackson Personal Injury and Costs Reforms’ by Andrew Mckie
‘A Guide to Consent in Clinical Negligence Post-Montgomery’ by Lauren Sutherland QC
‘A Practical Guide to Running Housing Disrepair and Cavity Wall Claims: 2nd Edition’ by Andrew Mckie & Ian Skeate
‘A Practical Guide to Digital and Social Media Law for Lawyers’ by Sherree Westell
‘A Practical Guide to Holiday Sickness Claims – 2nd Edition’ by Andrew Mckie & Ian Skeate
‘A Practical Guide to Elderly Law’ by Justin Patten
‘Arguments and Tactics for Personal Injury and Clinical Negligence Claims’ by Dorian Williams
‘A Practical Guide to QOCS and Fundamental Dishonesty’ by James Bentley
‘A Practical Guide to Drone Law’ by Rufus Ballaster, Andrew Firman, Eleanor Clot
‘Practical Mediation: A Guide for Mediators, Advocates, Advisers, Lawyers, and Students in Civil, Commercial, Business, Property, Workplace, and Employment Cases’ by Jonathan Dingle with John Sephton
‘A Comparative Guide to Standard Form Construction and Engineering Contracts’ by Jon Close
‘A Practical Guide to Compliance for Personal Injury Firms Working With Claims Management Companies’ by Paul Bennett
‘A Practical Guide to the Landlord and Tenant Act 1954: Commercial Tenancies’ by Richard Hayes & David Sawtell
‘A Practical Guide to Psychiatric Claims in Personal Injury’ by Liam Ryan
‘A Practical Guide to Dog Law for Owners and Others’ by Andrea Pitt

www.ingramcontent.com/pod-product-compliance
Ingram Content Group UK Ltd.
Pitfield, Milton Keynes, MK11 3LW, UK
UKHW020150290926
15471UKWH00004B/790

9 781912 687077